George Armstrong Custer

by Dana Meachen Rau

Compass Point Early Biographies

Content Adviser: Rodney G. Thomas, Colonel, U.S. Army (Retired),
Internet Editor, Custer Battlefield Historical and Museum Association

Reading Adviser: Dr. Linda D. Labbo,
Department of Reading Education, College of Education,
The University of Georgia

COMPASS POINT BOOKS

Minneapolis, Minnesota

Compass Point Books
3109 West 50th Street, #115
Minneapolis, MN 55410

Visit Compass Point Books on the Internet at *www.compasspointbooks.com*
or e-mail your request to *custserv@compasspointbooks.com*

Photographs ©: Denver Public Library, Western History Collection, cover, 22; Photo Sphere, cover background; Ohio Historical Society, 3
(top), 6; Courtesy Little Bighorn Battlefield National Monument/National Park Service, 3 (middle); Hulton/Archive by Getty Images, 3
(middle), 7, 8, 10, 13 (bottom); North Wind Picture Archives, 3 (bottom), 14 (top), 15, 17, 19, 25; Corbis, 4, 12; Bettmann/Corbis, 9;
Massachusetts Commandery Military Order of the Loyal Legion and the U.S. Army Military History Institute, 11, 13 (top); Stock Montage, 14
(bottom), 16, 20; "Gold Seekers to the Black Hills" by Howard Terpning, 2002, licensed by The Greenwich Workshop, Inc., 18; Woolaroc
Museum, Bartlesville, Oklahoma, 21; Buddy Mays/Corbis, 26.

Editors: E. Russell Primm, Emily J. Dolbear, and Catherine Neitge
Photo Researcher: Svetlana Zhurkina
Photo Selector: Linda S. Koutris
Designer/Page Production: Bradfordesign, Inc./Erin Scott, SARIN creative

Library of Congress Cataloging-in-Publication Data
Rau, Dana Meachen, 1971–
   George Armstrong Custer / by Dana Rau.
       p. cm.— (Compass Point early biographies)
Summary: A brief biography of the personal life, military career, and controversial accomplish-
ments of this legend in American history. Includes bibliographical references and index.
Contents: Growing up in Ohio—Training to be a soldier—The army life—The move west-
ward—Fighting the American Indians—The battle of Little Bighorn—Remembering the
"Indian fighter"—Important dates in Custer's life.
   ISBN 0-7565-0419-8 (Hardcover)
   1. Custer, George Armstrong, 1839–1876—Juvenile literature. 2. Generals—United States—
Biography—Juvenile literature. 3. United States. Army—Biography—Juvenile literature. 4.
Little Bighorn, Battle of the, Mont., 1876—Juvenile literature. [1. Custer, George Armstrong,
1839–1876. 2. Generals.] I. Title. II. Series.
   E467.1.C99 R34 2003
   973.8'2'092—dc21   2002009920

Table of Contents

*Note: In this book, words that are defined in the glossary are in **bold** the first time they appear in the text.*

Growing Up in Ohio

Legends are stories that people have told many times throughout history. The story of George Armstrong Custer has become a legend in the United States. He fought in the American Civil War (1861–1865) and in the West. He was a brave soldier.

George Armstrong Custer was born in New Rumley, Ohio, on December 5, 1839. He lived there on a farm with his parents, Emanuel and Marie. George often took care of horses. He learned to ride them, too.

In school, George was not a good student. He did not do his homework.

George Armstrong Custer

He played jokes on people instead. His parents sent him to live with his older sister and her husband in Monroe, Michigan, for three years. Then in 1855, George returned to New Rumley.

Training to Be a Soldier

George worked as a teacher in 1856, but he really wanted to be a soldier. So the next year, he entered the U.S. school for army training at West Point, New York.

Custer continued to get in trouble even at West Point.

George was always getting into trouble. Many of the boys at the school liked him, though. His height, his curly blond hair, and his blue eyes made everyone notice him.

◀ Custer's birthplace in New Rumley, Ohio

Students of West Point

　　While George was at West Point, the
United States was having big problems.
Everyone was sure a war was about to begin.
Southern states depended on the use of slaves

Slaves at work on a plantation

for farming. These slaves were people who had been taken from their homes in Africa. They were forced to work on large Southern farms called **plantations**. Northern states did not depend on slavery. Most people in the North thought slavery was wrong.

The American Civil War began in April

1861. George and the other young men in his class **graduated** early so they could fight. Then George went to Washington, D.C., to become a soldier.

Army Life

Custer fought for the Northern armies. Right away, he

Custer (left) with a fellow Northern officer during the Civil War

showed that he was a brave soldier. He was afraid of nothing. Custer fought in a cavalry unit. A cavalry is a group of soldiers who ride into battle on horses. Young Custer became a **general** when he was only twenty-three. He was in charge of about 2,500 men. He was also the youngest general in the Northern army. Some people called him the Boy General.

◄ The Civil War broke out while Custer was studying at West Point.

Custer was called
the Boy General.

During a break from fighting, General Custer went to Monroe, Michigan. He visited Elizabeth Bacon, a woman he had met a few years earlier. He liked her very much. They were married in 1864. Elizabeth often worried about him during battles.

The Civil War ended in 1865. General Custer had proved to be a great soldier and leader. Now he was ready for something new. He would go West.

Wagon trains of settlers, like Custer, ▶
headed West for a new life.

The Move Westward

During the 1800s, many people from the eastern United States moved westward. The West had lots of unsettled land.

Elizabeth Bacon Custer

People looking for a new life moved there to build homes and farm the land. But thousands

Many Americans wanted to move West because they knew it had rich, unsettled farm land.

of Native Americans already lived on that land. Many had never even seen white people, and the white people did not understand the Indians. The whites wanted to settle the land.

Native Americans were living in the West long before white settlers moved into that area.

14

They did not care
that Indians had been
living there for thou-
sands of years. The
U.S. government then
set aside certain
areas of land called
reservations for the
Native Americans to

Native Americans did not want to move to reservations.

live on. The Indians did not want to move
there. Many of them refused to go. The U.S.
government then sent General Custer and
other soldiers to the West to deal with the
problem.

Fighting the Native Americans

In 1866, Custer and his men were sent to Kansas to fight. Custer's many victories during the Civil War made him famous. It was believed that he would be a great Indian fighter.

Battles between whites and Native Americans were fierce and bloody.

In 1873, Custer and his men were sent to Dakota Territory. The white people there wanted to build a railroad across Indian land. Many white settlers were moving in to the newly acquired lands. Custer was sent there to protect the settlers from the Indians and the Indians from the settlers.

Custer's job was also to keep out **miners** who went to the Black Hills in

◄ Government troops attacked the Snake River Indians.

Dakota Territory to dig for gold. This proved to be impossible. The Black Hills were a very special place to the Native Americans. Sitting Bull, Crazy Horse, and other Native American chiefs were unhappy and angry when the miners arrived. Some led attacks on the miners.

The Battle of the Little Bighorn

The U.S. government kept trying to force all the Indians to live on reservations. Most Indians did not want to do this. The government decided to use the army to force the Indians onto the reservations.

The U.S. government forced many Native Americans to move to reservations.

Custer and his men were sent by the army to find the Indian camps. The army sent three groups out to look for the Indians.

◄ Native Americans had to deal with white miners eager to explore the Black Hills for gold.

Custer's troops had to find the location of the larger Native American camps.

In about a month they had found where the larger Indian villages were set up.

Custer had **scouts** working for him. These scouts were Indians who knew the land and helped guide the soldiers.

Sitting Bull was one of the Native American leaders who did not ➤ want the government to remove his people from their lands.

On June 25, 1876, the scouts spotted a large camp of Lakota and Cheyenne Indians near the Little Bighorn River in Montana Territory.

Custer thought he and his troops would be able to fight the Indians easily. He had more than two hundred men. Custer, like the rest of the army leaders, thought they could force the Indians onto the reservations without much trouble. Custer split his unit into smaller units. The Indians surrounded them and killed them. The Indians were led by Sitting Bull, Crazy Horse, Gall, and Lame White Man. Custer and all his soliders were killed in the battle that followed.

◄ Curley, one of Custer's Indian scouts, was the only army member to survive the bloody battle.

Remembering the Legend

For many years after Custer died, Americans called that battle "Custer's Last Stand." People wrote plays and books about the Battle of the Little Bighorn. They also made movies and painted pictures about Custer. They believed he was a hero.

Today, people have many different thoughts about Custer. Some think he was brave. Others think he made many mistakes. Some think he should have waited for more soldiers to arrive and help with the fighting. Also, many people believe the U.S. government

The famous battle became known as "Custer's Last Stand." ➤

was unfair to take away land from the Native Americans. They believe the Native Americans were right to fight back. No matter what people think of Custer, however, he was an important person in American history.

The field next to the Little Bighorn River was made a national **monument** in 1946. It was called the Custer Battlefield National Monument until 1991. Now it is called the Little Bighorn Battlefield National Monument. Thousands of people visit the battlefield each year to honor the Indians and soldiers who died during the battle.

◄ Gravestones at Little Bighorn Battlefield National Monument remind visitors of the many lives lost near the Little Bighorn River.

Important Dates in George Armstrong Custer's Life

1839 — Born on December 5 in New Rumley, Ohio

1853–1855 — Lives with his sister and her husband in Monroe, Michigan

1856 — Works as a teacher in Ohio

1857–1861 — Attends the United States Military Academy at West Point, New York

1861–1865 — The Northern states fight the Southern states in the Civil War

1863 — Custer becomes the youngest general in the Northern army

1864 — Marries Elizabeth Bacon on February 9

1866 — Sent to Kansas to fight Native Americans

1873 — Sent to Dakota Territory to protect railroad workers from attacks by Native Americans

1874 — Gold is discovered in the Black Hills of Dakota Territory

1876 — Custer and his men are all killed in the Battle of the Little Bighorn on June 25

1877 — Custer's body is buried at the United States Military Academy at West Point, New York

1946 — The Little Bighorn Battlefield in Montana becomes the Custer Battlefield National Monument

1991 — The Little Bighorn Battlefield National Monument is established

Glossary

general—an officer of the highest rank in the army

graduated—finished school

legends—stories passed down through the years that may not be completely true

miners—people who dig for gold or other metals

monument—a statue or an area set aside to honor an event or a person

plantations—large farms where crops such as cotton were grown

reservations—large areas of land set aside for Native Americans

scouts—people who know an area well and are sent by soldiers to see what is ahead

Did You Know?

- As a child, George Armstrong Custer pronounced his middle name as "Autie." It became his nickname growing up.

- During the Civil War, Custer scouted the enemy by flying in a hot-air balloon.

- Custer fought in many battles during the Civil War, but he was wounded only once.

Want to Know More?

At the Library

Bruchac, Joseph. *Crazy Horse's Vision*. New York: Lee and Low Books, 2000.

Cooper, Jason. *Little Bighorn Battlefield*. Vero Beach, Fla.: Rourke, 2000.

Kent, Zachary. *George Armstrong Custer: Civil War and Western Legend*. Springfield, N.J.: Enslow Publishers, Inc., 2000.

Press, Petra. *The Sioux*. Minneapolis: Compass Point Books, 2001.

On the Web

Custer's Short Biography
http://www.civilwarhome.com/custerbi.htm
For highlights of Custer's Civil War record

Through the Mail

Custer Memorial
Custer Memorial Association
46320 Cadiz-Junction Road
Hopedale, OH 43976
740/946-3781
To get more information about Custer's life and military career

On the Road

Little Bighorn Battlefield National Monument
P.O. Box 39
Crow Agency, MT 59022
406/638-2621
To learn more about the battle and to visit the place where Custer was killed

Index

About the Author

Dana Meachen Rau is a children's book author, editor, and illustrator. She has written more than seventy-five books, including nonfiction, biographies, early readers, and historical fiction. She is a graduate of Trinity College in Hartford, Connecticut. Dana works from her home office in Burlington, Connecticut, where she lives with her husband, Chris, and children, Charlie and Allison.